# Extra! Extra! Read All About It

Adrian Rocquecliffe

Published by Writers Sidekick Publishing, 2024.

EXTRA! EXTRA! READ ALL ABOUT IT

**First edition. July 6, 2024.**



ISBN: 979-8227044839

Written by Adrian Rocquecliffe.

# FAKE NEWS

"Fake News" has become a pervasive term in contemporary discourse, referring to false or misleading information presented as legitimate news. Let's delve deeper into the concept, its origins, impact, and strategies for combatting misinformation.

## Origins

The phrase "Fake News" gained widespread popularity during and after the 2016 United States presidential election, notably when then-candidate Donald Trump used it to dismiss critical coverage and allegations against him. Trump frequently employed the term "Fake News" to discredit media outlets that reported unfavorably on his campaign or administration, often referring to mainstream news organizations as purveyors of false or biased information.

While Trump did not coin the term "Fake News," his frequent use on social media and public statements contributed to its mainstream usage and cultural significance, by labeling unfavorable news coverage as "Fake News," Trump sought to undermine the credibility of the media and deflect criticism, framing negative stories as partisan attacks or attempts to delegitimize his presidency.

It's important to note that the term "Fake News" has since evolved beyond its original context. It is now commonly used to describe a broader phenomenon of false or misleading information spread across various platforms and by various actors. However, Trump's use of the phrase during the 2016 election campaign played a significant role in popularizing it as a catch-all term for discrediting unfavorable media coverage.

However, the roots of intentionally deceptive or manipulative news can be traced back in history.

## Pre-Digital Age

Even before the advent of the internet and social media, deceptive news practices were prevalent. In the late 19th and early 20th centuries, newspapers engaged in sensationalized reporting, known as yellow journalism, characterized by exaggerated headlines, lurid stories, and sensationalized imagery designed to attract readership and boost sales. Publishers such as William Randolph Hearst and Joseph Pulitzer were infamous for using sensationalism to manipulate public opinion and advance their political agendas.

## Propaganda

Throughout history, governments and political actors have used propaganda to shape public perceptions and influence behavior. Propaganda campaigns can involve disseminating false or misleading information to promote a particular agenda or ideology, often through mass media channels such as newspapers, radio, television, and now, the internet. During war or political upheaval, propaganda has been used to demonize enemies, rally support for government policies, and manipulate public opinion.

## Tabloid Sensationalism

In popular media, tabloid newspapers and magazines have long been criticized for their sensationalized and often fabricated stories. Tabloids thrive on scandal, gossip, and sensationalism, prioritizing entertainment value over journalistic integrity. While tabloid journalism may not always be explicitly political, it contributes to the broader culture of sensationalism and misinformation that can erode public trust in the media.

## Digital Age

The proliferation of the internet and social media platforms in the late 20th and early 21st centuries dramatically transformed the landscape of news dissemination. While these technologies have democratized access to information and empowered individuals to share news and opinions globally, they have also facilitated the spread of misinformation and disinformation. Social media algorithms prioritize engagement and virality, incentivizing the spread of sensational or provocative content, regardless of its accuracy or veracity. This phenomenon has been exacerbated by the rise of clickbait headlines, Fake News websites, and echo chambers, where individuals are exposed only to information that reinforces their existing beliefs.

Various actors can implement Fake News for many reasons, often to deceive, manipulate, or achieve specific objectives. Here are some key actors who may implement Fake News and their motivations

## Foreign Governments

Foreign governments may engage in disseminating Fake News as part of broader disinformation campaigns aimed at undermining rival nations, sowing discord, or advancing geopolitical interests. For example, state-sponsored troll farms and media outlets may spread false information to influence public opinion, destabilize democratic institutions, or create confusion and division within target countries.

## Political Parties and Candidates

Political parties and candidates may utilize Fake News to gain a strategic advantage in elections, discredit opponents, or shape public perceptions of critical issues. False or misleading information may be circulated to mobilize supporters, suppress voter turnout, or exploit societal divisions for political gain.

## Special Interest Groups

Special interest groups, including advocacy organizations, corporations, and ideological movements, may employ Fake News to promote their agendas, discredit adversaries, or advance specific policy objectives. Misinformation campaigns funded by vested interests may aim to shape public opinion, influence legislation, or undermine regulatory efforts that threaten their interests.

## Clickbait Websites and Content Farms

Some individuals or organizations may create Fake News content for financial gain, exploiting clickbait tactics to drive website traffic and generate advertising revenue. Regardless of their accuracy or veracity, content farms may churn out sensationalized or fabricated stories designed to go viral on social media platforms.

## Social Media Users

Individual users of social media platforms may unknowingly or deliberately share Fake News stories, contributing to the spread of misinformation online. Factors such as confirmation bias, cognitive dissonance, and the desire for social validation can incentivize users to share content that aligns with their beliefs or elicits solid emotional reactions without critically evaluating its accuracy or credibility.

## Malign Actors and Hackers

Malign actors, including cybercriminals, hacktivists, and online trolls, may disseminate Fake News as part of cyber attacks, information warfare, or online harassment campaigns. False information may be weaponized to undermine trust in institutions, sow chaos, or manipulate public sentiment in pursuit of malicious objectives.

## Satirical or Parody Websites

While not necessarily malicious, satirical or parody websites may publish Fake News stories for entertainment or comedic purposes. However, unsuspecting readers can sometimes misinterpret these stories as genuine news, leading to confusion or misinformation.

Implementing Fake News can serve various purposes, from geopolitical manipulation and political propaganda to financial profit and online entertainment. Understanding the motivations behind Fake News dissemination is essential for developing effective strategies to combat misinformation and safeguard the integrity of public discourse.

# Impact

The impact of Fake News extends far beyond the dissemination of false or misleading information, with implications for trust in the media, public discourse, and democratic processes. Here's an elaboration on its impact

## Erosion Of Trust In The Media

Fake News undermines trust in traditional media sources and institutions as audiences become increasingly skeptical of the reliability and credibility of news outlets. When misinformation is presented alongside legitimate reporting, it can blur the lines between fact and fiction, making it difficult for audiences to discern truth from falsehood.

## Distortion of Public Discourse

The proliferation of Fake News distorts public discourse by injecting false narratives and sensationalized stories into the public sphere. Misinformation can shape public perceptions, influence public opinion, and distort policy debates, leading to a misinformed electorate and hindering democratic decision-making.

## Influence on Political Attitudes and Behaviors

Fake News can influence political attitudes and behaviors by shaping individuals' perceptions of political issues, candidates, and parties. False or misleading information can sway voter opinions, reinforce existing biases, and fuel polarization, leading to increased ideological divisions and decreased willingness to engage in civil discourse.

## Amplification through Social Media

Social media platforms have amplified the impact of Fake News by providing a global distribution network for false information. Algorithms that prioritize engagement and virality can inadvertently promote sensational or provocative content, leading to the rapid spread of misinformation and making it challenging to counteract false narratives once they gain traction.

## Contribution to Social Polarization

Fake News has been linked to social polarization, as individuals are exposed to information reinforcing their beliefs and biases. Echo chambers and filter bubbles on social media platforms can exacerbate ideological divisions, reduce exposure to diverse perspectives, and hinder constructive dialogue and compromise on contentious issues.

## Propagation of Conspiracy Theories

Fake News often fuels the spread of conspiracy theories and fringe beliefs as individuals seek to make sense of complex or uncertain events. False information can validate existing conspiracy narratives, leading to the proliferation of baseless claims, mistrust in institutions, and the erosion of consensus reality.

## Threat to Democratic Norms and Institutions

The spread of Fake News threatens democratic norms and institutions by undermining public trust in electoral processes, government institutions, and the rule of law. Disinformation campaigns can sow doubt about the legitimacy of democratic elections, weaken democratic institutions, and create opportunities for authoritarian leaders to exploit political instability.

In summary, Fake News has far-reaching consequences that extend beyond information dissemination, affecting trust in the media, public discourse, political attitudes and behaviors, social cohesion, and democratic governance. Addressing the challenges posed by Fake News requires concerted efforts from governments, technology companies, civil society organizations, and individuals to promote media literacy, combat Misinformation, and safeguard the integrity of public discourse and democratic processes.

# Forms

Fake News encompasses a wide range of deceptive and misleading content that can take various forms, each with its characteristics and implications. Here's an elaboration on the forms of Fake News

## Fabricated Stories

Fabricated stories are entirely false narratives created to deceive readers or viewers. These stories often mimic the style and format of legitimate news articles containing fictional events, quotes, and sources. Fabricated stories may be designed to elicit strong emotional reactions or reinforce existing biases, making them more likely to be shared widely on social media platforms.

## Doctored Images or Videos

Fake News can also involve manipulating images or videos to convey false information or misrepresent events. Doctored images may be altered using photo editing software to create misleading visuals. In contrast, deepfake videos use artificial intelligence technology to superimpose individuals' faces onto existing footage, making it appear like they are saying or doing things they never actually did.

## Misleading Headlines

Misleading headlines are another common form of Fake News, where an article or social media post headline is crafted to grab attention and generate clicks, even if the content itself is accurate or balanced. Sensationalized or exaggerated headlines can distort the true nature of a story, leading readers to draw false conclusions or share misinformation without reading the full article.

## Biased Reporting

Fake News may also involve biased reporting, where journalists or media outlets selectively present information to advance a particular agenda or ideology. Biased reporting can involve omitting relevant facts, cherry-picking quotes, or framing stories to favor one side of an issue while disregarding opposing viewpoints. This form of Fake News can be subtle and difficult to detect, as it often involves manipulation of tone, language, and framing rather than outright falsehoods.

## Financially Motivated Content

Some Fake News sites are created for financial gain, with creators exploiting clickbait tactics to generate advertising revenue. Content farms and clickbait websites churn out sensationalized or fabricated stories designed to attract clicks and views, regardless of their accuracy or veracity. These websites prioritize engagement metrics over journalistic integrity, contributing to the spread of misinformation and disinformation online.

## Ideological or Political Propaganda

Fake News may also be disseminated for ideological or political purposes to manipulate public opinion, sow discord, or advance specific agendas. Partisan actors, foreign governments, and special interest groups may employ disinformation tactics to discredit adversaries, shape public perceptions, or influence electoral outcomes. Ideologically driven Fake News may exploit existing social divisions, promote conspiracy theories, or demonize political opponents to achieve strategic objectives.

In summary, Fake News can manifest in various forms, each with its motivations and implications. Whether it's fabricated stories, doctored images or videos, misleading headlines, biased reporting, financially motivated content, or ideological propaganda, the spread of Fake News poses significant challenges to media literacy, public trust, and democratic discourse. Recognizing and combating these different forms of Fake News requires a multifaceted approach that involves media literacy education, fact-checking initiatives, technological interventions, and regulatory measures to promote the integrity of information ecosystems and safeguard democratic processes.

# Combatting Misinformation

Combatting misinformation is essential to safeguarding the integrity of public discourse and democratic processes. Here's an elaboration on strategies for addressing the spread of Fake News

## Media Literacy Education

Educating the public about media literacy and critical thinking skills is crucial for empowering individuals to discern credible information from misinformation. Media literacy programs can teach people how to evaluate sources, identify bias, fact-check claims, and critically analyze news stories before sharing them. By promoting digital literacy and responsible information consumption habits, media literacy education helps individuals become more discerning consumers of news and information.

## Fact-Checking Initiatives

Fact-checking organizations play a critical role in combatting misinformation by verifying the accuracy of claims and debunking false information. These organizations employ rigorous research methods and evidence-based analysis to assess the truthfulness of statements made by politicians, public figures, and news sources. By providing transparent and impartial claims assessments, fact-checkers help counteract the spread of false narratives and promote informed public discourse.

## Technological Solutions

Social media platforms and technology companies have implemented various measures to combat the spread of Fake News on their platforms. This includes algorithms that prioritize credible sources, demote or remove misleading content, and features that flag disputed or potentially false information. Additionally, platforms may partner with fact-checking organizations to provide users with additional context and verification when encountering questionable content.

## User Empowerment Tools

Empowering users with tools and features to identify and report misinformation can help mitigate its impact. Social media platforms may allow users to flag suspicious content, report Fake News stories, or access fact-checking resources directly within the platform. Encouraging users to evaluate information and engage in responsible sharing practices critically can help prevent the inadvertent spread of false information.

## Regulatory Measures

Governments and policymakers may implement regulatory measures to address the spread of Fake News, such as laws or regulations governing online content moderation, transparency requirements for social media platforms, and penalties for disseminating false information with malicious intent. While regulatory interventions must balance concerns around free speech and censorship, targeted measures to combat misinformation can help promote accountability and responsibility among online actors.

Overall, combatting misinformation requires a collaborative effort involving media literacy education, fact-checking initiatives, technological solutions, and regulatory measures. By empowering individuals to critically evaluate information, holding purveyors of Fake News accountable, and promoting transparency and integrity in information ecosystems, society can better protect the integrity of public discourse and democratic processes in the digital age.

# Ethical Journalism

Ethical journalism is a critical bulwark against the spread of Fake News, ensuring that accurate and reliable information reaches the public. Here's an elaboration on the principles of ethical journalism

## Verification

Ethical journalists prioritize the verification of information before publishing or broadcasting stories. This involves corroborating facts with multiple sources, cross-checking information for accuracy, and verifying the credibility of sources. Journalists can guard against disseminating false or misleading information by fact-checking claims and statements.

## Accuracy

Accuracy is paramount in ethical journalism, as inaccuracies can erode trust and undermine the credibility of news organizations. Journalists report information truthfully and objectively, avoiding errors, misrepresentations, and distortions. Verifying facts, confirming details, and correcting errors - promptly are essential practices for maintaining accuracy in reporting.

## Fairness and Impartiality

Ethical journalists adhere to principles of fairness and impartiality in their reporting, striving to present diverse perspectives and avoid bias or prejudice. This involves providing balanced coverage of events, giving voice to all relevant stakeholders, and refraining from favoritism or partisanship. Fair and impartial reporting helps foster trust with audiences and ensures that news coverage reflects a broad range of viewpoints.

## Transparency

Transparency is a core tenet of ethical journalism, as it fosters accountability and trust between journalists and audiences. Journalists should be transparent about their sources, methods, and motivations, disclosing any conflicts of interest or biases that may influence their reporting. Providing context, attribution, and background information helps audiences evaluate the reliability and credibility of news stories.

## Independence

Ethical journalists maintain independence from outside influences, including advertisers, political parties, and special interests. They uphold editorial autonomy and resist undue pressure or interference that may compromise the integrity of their reporting. Journalists can uphold their duty to serve the public interest and hold power to account by maintaining editorial independence.

## Sensitivity and Responsibility

Ethical journalists exercise sensitivity and responsibility in their reporting, considering the potential impact of their coverage on individuals and communities. They avoid sensationalism, gratuitous violence, and invasion of privacy, prioritizing the dignity and well-being of those affected by their reporting. Responsible journalism seeks to inform, educate, and empower audiences while minimizing harm and respecting ethical boundaries.

In summary, ethical journalism plays a vital role in combatting Fake News by upholding principles of verification, accuracy, fairness, impartiality, transparency, independence, sensitivity, and responsibility. By adhering to these ethical standards, journalists can be trusted guardians of truth and integrity, providing audiences with reliable information and fostering informed public discourse.

# Psychological Factors

Psychological factors play a significant role in the dissemination and reception of Fake News, shaping how individuals perceive, interpret, and share information. Here's an elaboration on some fundamental psychological mechanisms

## Confirmation Bias

Confirmation bias refers to the tendency for individuals to seek out, interpret, and recall information in a way that confirms their existing beliefs or biases while disregarding contradictory evidence. When exposed to Fake News that aligns with their preconceived notions or ideological leanings, people are more likely to accept it uncritically and share it with others, reinforcing their beliefs and preferences.

## Illusion of Truth Effect

The illusion of truth effect is when people are more likely to believe false information after repeated exposure, even if initially skeptical. This cognitive bias stems from the idea that familiarity breeds credibility, leading individuals to mistake familiarity for accuracy. As Fake News stories are circulated and shared across social media platforms, they gain an aura of credibility through repetition, making them more persuasive to unsuspecting audiences.

## Viral Nature of Social Media

Social media platforms amplify the spread of Fake News through their viral nature, enabling misinformation to reach a broad audience rapidly. Algorithms that prioritize engaging or sensational content and users' tendency to share content that resonates with their emotions or beliefs create echo chambers where false information circulates unchecked among like-minded groups. This echo chamber effect reinforces ideological polarization and exacerbates the spread of misinformation within online communities.

## Emotional Appeals

Fake News often leverages emotional appeals to capture attention and elicit strong audience reactions. Stories that evoke fear, outrage, or sympathy are more likely to be shared virally, as they trigger emotional responses that override rational skepticism. By tapping into people's emotions, Fake News exploits psychological vulnerabilities. It increases its likelihood of being disseminated widely across social networks.

## Selective Exposure

Selective exposure refers to individuals' tendency to seek information that aligns with their beliefs or preferences while avoiding information that contradicts them. In an era of personalized news feeds and filter bubbles, people are increasingly exposed to content that reinforces their worldview, making them more susceptible to Fake News that reinforces their biases and prejudices.

By understanding these psychological factors, researchers, journalists, and policymakers can develop more effective strategies for combatting the spread of Fake News. Educating the public about cognitive biases, promoting critical thinking skills, improving media literacy, and fostering diverse and inclusive online communities are essential steps in mitigating the impact of Fake News on society. Additionally, social media platforms can implement measures to mitigate the viral spread of misinformation, such as fact-checking labels, content moderation policies, and algorithmic adjustments to reduce echo chamber effects and promote information diversity.

# Global Impact

The global impact of Fake News is profound, transcending national boundaries and affecting societies worldwide. Here's an evaluation of its implications

## Cross-Border Dissemination

With the proliferation of digital communication technologies and social media platforms, Fake News can spread rapidly across borders, reaching audiences in diverse countries and regions. Misinformation campaigns originating in one country can influence public opinion, shape political discourse, and undermine trust in institutions worldwide. The internet's borderless nature enables malicious actors to exploit vulnerabilities in information ecosystems, amplifying the global impact of Fake News.

## Political Polarization

Fake News contributes to political polarization and social divisions on a global scale by promoting divisive narratives, fostering distrust in mainstream media, and deepening ideological rifts within societies. In democracies, spreading false information can undermine public confidence in electoral processes, fuel partisan animosity, and erode democratic norms and institutions. Authoritarian regimes may weaponize Fake News to suppress dissent, control public discourse, and manipulate public opinion to consolidate power.

## Public Health and Safety

Misinformation poses significant risks to public health and safety, particularly during crises such as pandemics, natural disasters, and public health emergencies. False information about vaccines, treatments, and preventive measures can undermine public trust in health authorities, exacerbate vaccine hesitancy, and contribute to the spread of preventable diseases. During emergencies, misinformation can impede practical response efforts, endangering lives and exacerbating the impact of disasters.

## Economic Consequences

The proliferation of Fake News can have economic consequences at both the individual and societal levels. Disinformation campaigns targeting businesses, financial markets, or consumer products can manipulate market sentiment, disrupt supply chains, and undermine investor confidence, leading to financial losses and economic instability. Moreover, the erosion of trust in online information sources can undermine the digital economy by reducing consumer confidence in online transactions and e-commerce platforms.

## International Cooperation

Addressing the global impact of Fake News requires international cooperation and collaboration among governments, technology companies, civil society organizations, and international institutions.

Combating misinformation must involve sharing best practices, exchanging information, coordinating regulatory frameworks, and developing joint strategies to counter disinformation campaigns. International agreements and initiatives promoting media literacy, digital literacy, and online safety can help build resilience against Fake News and strengthen global efforts to safeguard the integrity of information ecosystems.

In conclusion, the global impact of Fake News underscores the need for concerted action at the national, regional, and international levels to address this multifaceted challenge. By promoting media literacy, enhancing transparency and accountability in online information environments, and fostering international cooperation, stakeholders can mitigate the harmful effects of Fake News and uphold the principles of truth, integrity, and democracy in the digital age.

# Legal And Regulatory Challenges

Addressing the legal and regulatory challenges posed by Fake News requires careful consideration of the complex interplay between combating misinformation and upholding principles of free speech and expression. Here's an elaboration on these challenges

## Censorship Concerns

Laws and regulations to curb the spread of Fake News often raise concerns about censorship and government overreach. Governments may use anti-Fake News legislation as a pretext to suppress dissent, silence political opponents, or restrict freedom of expression. Critics argue that vague or overly broad legal definitions of Fake News can be exploited to target legitimate journalism, independent media outlets, and dissenting voices, undermining press freedom and democratic rights.

## Impact on Media Freedom

Legal and regulatory measures to combat Fake News can have unintended consequences for media freedom and editorial independence. Journalists and media organizations may self-censor or avoid covering controversial topics for fear of violating anti-Fake News laws or facing legal repercussions. Such chilling effects can undermine investigative journalism, hinder public access to information, and diminish media pluralism, stifling democratic debate and accountability.

## Freedom of Expression

Safeguarding freedom of expression is essential in democratic societies, as it enables individuals to express diverse viewpoints, engage in public debate, and hold power to account. Restrictions on speech, even those aimed at combating Fake News, must be narrowly tailored, proportionate, and consistent with international human rights standards. Balancing the need to combat misinformation with the protection of free speech requires careful calibration of legal and regulatory frameworks to prevent abuse and protect fundamental rights.

## Transnational Challenges

The internet's borderless nature presents challenges for regulating Fake News, as disinformation campaigns can originate from anywhere in the world and target audiences across multiple jurisdictions. Coordination among countries is essential to address transnational threats from Fake News effectively. However, differences in legal systems, cultural norms, and political contexts can complicate efforts to harmonize regulatory approaches and promote international cooperation in combating misinformation.

## Role of Technology Companies

Technology companies play a pivotal role in combating Fake News by implementing content moderation policies, fact-checking initiatives, and algorithmic adjustments to reduce the spread of misinformation on their platforms. However, questions remain about the accountability, transparency, and effectiveness of private sector measures in addressing the root causes of Fake News. Collaborative efforts between governments, civil society, and tech companies are needed to develop comprehensive strategies for combating misinformation while respecting fundamental rights and democratic values.

In conclusion, navigating the legal and regulatory challenges posed by Fake News requires a nuanced approach that balances the imperative to combat misinformation with the protection of free speech and expression. Effective strategies must uphold democratic principles, ensure transparency and accountability in regulatory processes, and promote collaboration among stakeholders to safeguard the integrity of public discourse and information ecosystems.

# Role Of Technology

Technology's role in spreading and mitigating Fake News is multifaceted, encompassing challenges and opportunities. Here's an elaboration on its various aspects

## Facilitation of Dissemination

Social media platforms and digital technologies have democratized access to information, enabling individuals to share news and opinions instantaneously with a global audience. However, this interconnectedness has also created fertile ground for rapidly disseminating false or misleading information. Misformation can spread virally across online networks, bypassing traditional gatekeepers and fact-checking mechanisms.

## Algorithmic Amplification

The algorithms powering social media platforms and search engines play a significant role in amplifying the reach and visibility of content, including Fake News. These algorithms prioritize engagement metrics such as likes, shares, and comments, often promoting sensational or polarizing content that generates high levels of user interaction. As a result, false information may be algorithmically amplified, leading to its widespread dissemination and increased susceptibility to viral spread.

## Content Moderation

Technology companies have implemented various content moderation measures to combat Fake News, including automated systems, human reviewers, and community reporting mechanisms. These efforts aim to identify and remove false or harmful content from online platforms, mitigating its impact on users. However, content moderation practices face challenges such as scale, accuracy, and consistency, as the sheer volume of user-generated content makes it difficult to detect and address every instance of Fake News effectively.

## Fact-Checking Tools

Technology-driven fact-checking initiatives leverage artificial intelligence and natural language processing techniques to assess the credibility and accuracy of online information. Fact-checking organizations and independent researchers use automated tools and manual verification processes to evaluate claims, identify misinformation, and provide accurate context and corrections. These fact-checking efforts help debunk false narratives, inform public discourse, and promote media literacy among online users.

## Media Literacy Education

Technology can also facilitate media literacy education and critical thinking skills development through digital tools, online resources, and educational platforms. Media literacy initiatives empower individuals to discern credible sources from misinformation, critically evaluate information, and navigate online environments responsibly. By promoting digital literacy and critical media consumption habits, technology can help inoculate users against the influence of Fake News and disinformation.

## Ethical Considerations

While technology offers promising solutions for combating Fake News, ethical considerations must guide its development and deployment. Privacy, transparency, bias, and accountability require careful attention to ensure that technological interventions uphold democratic values, respect user rights, and mitigate unintended consequences. Collaborative efforts between technologists, policymakers, civil society, and academia are essential to address these ethical challenges effectively.

In conclusion, the role of technology in addressing Fake News encompasses a range of strategies and interventions, from algorithmic adjustments and content moderation to fact-checking tools and media literacy education. By harnessing the potential of technology responsibly and ethically, stakeholders can mitigate the harmful effects of Fake News and foster a more informed and resilient society in the digital age.

# Erosion Of Trust

The erosion of trust, exacerbated by the proliferation of Fake News, poses significant challenges to democratic societies and institutions. Here's an elaboration on how Fake News contributes to this phenomenon and strategies for rebuilding trust

## Impact on Media Trust

Fake News undermines public confidence in traditional media outlets and journalistic integrity. When false or misleading information is disseminated alongside credible news sources, it blurs the line between fact and fiction, making it difficult for audiences to discern trustworthy sources of information. As a result, skepticism toward mainstream media can increase, leading to a loss of trust in journalistic professionalism and ethical standards.

## Distrust in Government and Institutions

Fake News can also erode trust in government institutions and public officials. Misformation may manipulate public opinion, discredit political opponents, or sow discord. When citizens encounter false information from official sources or government representatives, it can fuel skepticism and disillusionment with the political process, undermining democratic legitimacy and accountability.

## Skepticism Toward Experts and Authorities

In addition to media and government, Fake News can diminish trust in experts, scientists, and other authoritative sources of information. Misinformation campaigns may target scientific consensus on climate change, public health, or national security, casting doubt on evidence-based policymaking and eroding public confidence in expertise. As a result, individuals may become more susceptible to conspiracy theories or fringe narratives that challenge established knowledge.

## Rebuilding Trust

Rebuilding trust in institutions requires a concerted effort to address the root causes of distrust and restore confidence in authoritative sources of information. Transparency and accountability are essential, as institutions must be open about their processes, decisions, and actions to regain public trust. Journalists and media organizations can prioritize accuracy, fact-checking, and ethical reporting practices to demonstrate their commitment to truth and integrity.

## Promoting Media Literacy

Educating the public about media literacy and critical thinking skills is crucial in combating the spread of Fake News and misinformation. By equipping individuals with the tools to evaluate information critically, recognize bias, and verify sources, media literacy initiatives empower citizens to navigate an increasingly complex media landscape and make informed decisions about the information they consume and share.

## Regulating Social Media Platforms

Addressing the role of social media platforms in amplifying Fake News requires regulatory measures to promote transparency, accountability, and responsible content moderation. Technology companies must implement robust measures to detect and remove false information from their platforms. At the same time, governments can enact legislation to hold platforms accountable for their role in disseminating harmful content.

## Fostering Dialogue and Engagement

Rebuilding trust also fosters open dialogue, constructive engagement, and participatory governance processes involving citizens in decision-making and policy development. By promoting transparency, inclusivity, and responsiveness, institutions can demonstrate their commitment to democratic values and regain the public's confidence.

In conclusion, addressing the erosion of trust caused by Fake News requires a multifaceted approach that involves media organizations, governments, technology companies, and civil society working together to promote transparency, accountability, and integrity in the information ecosystem. By rebuilding trust in institutions and fostering a culture of critical thinking and media literacy, societies can confront the challenges posed by Fake News and strengthen democratic resilience in the digital age.

# Weaponization Of Information

The weaponization of information represents a significant challenge in the modern era, as Fake News and disinformation campaigns are increasingly employed as tools for political manipulation, social control, and geopolitical influence. Here's an elaboration on how information is weaponized and its implications

## Discrediting Political Opponents

Fake News can undermine the credibility and reputation of political opponents. By spreading false or misleading information about rival candidates or parties, political actors seek to tarnish their image, erode public trust, and sway voter perceptions. This tactic is particularly prevalent during elections, where disinformation campaigns aim to manipulate public opinion and influence electoral outcomes.

## Inciting Social Unrest

Fake News and inflammatory narratives can exploit societal divisions, amplify grievances, and incite social unrest. By disseminating divisive content targeting ethnic, religious, or ideological groups, malicious actors seek to exacerbate tensions, provoke conflict, and destabilize communities. Social media platforms provide fertile ground for the rapid spread of incendiary content, amplifying its impact and contributing to polarization and distrust.

## Destabilizing Foreign Governments

State-sponsored disinformation campaigns are often employed as a tool of geopolitical warfare to undermine foreign governments and sow discord within target countries. By spreading false narratives, amplifying conspiracy theories, and manipulating public opinion, hostile actors seek to weaken democratic institutions, erode public confidence in governance, and exploit vulnerabilities in the information ecosystem. These efforts may be aimed at fomenting unrest, subverting elections, or exerting influence over strategic decision-making processes.

## Cyber Warfare and Hybrid Threats

Information warfare encompasses a range of tactics, including cyber attacks, hacking, and social media manipulation, aimed at achieving strategic objectives in the digital domain. State and non-state actors may use cyber warfare and hybrid threats to disrupt communication networks, sabotage critical infrastructure, and undermine national security. Fake News and disinformation play a central role in these campaigns, serving as a means of psychological warfare and coercive diplomacy in the geopolitical arena.

## Implications for Democracy and Stability

The weaponization of information poses significant risks to democratic institutions, societal cohesion, and international security. By exploiting vulnerabilities in the information ecosystem, malicious actors can undermine the integrity of elections, manipulate public opinion, and destabilize governments, posing threats to democratic norms and principles. Moreover, the proliferation of Fake News and disinformation erodes trust in institutions, fosters polarization, and undermines social cohesion, weakening the fabric of democratic societies.

In conclusion, the weaponization of information represents a complex and multifaceted challenge with far-reaching implications for governance, security, and democracy. Addressing this phenomenon requires a concerted effort from governments, technology companies, civil society organizations, and international actors to counter disinformation, promote media literacy, and safeguard the integrity of the information ecosystem. By enhancing resilience to information warfare and defending against malicious manipulation, societies can mitigate the threats posed by the weaponization of information and uphold democratic values in the digital age.

# Deepfakes And Manipulated Media

Deepfake technology has ushered in a new era of concern regarding the authenticity and reliability of audio and video content. Deepfakes are digitally altered media, often using artificial intelligence (AI) algorithms to superimpose the likeness and voice of one person onto another realistically and convincingly. Here's an elaboration on Deepfakes and their implications

## Sophistication of Deepfake Technology

Deepfake technology has evolved rapidly, enabling the creation of highly realistic and convincing manipulated media. By leveraging machine learning algorithms and neural networks, creators can generate deepfake videos and audio recordings that seamlessly mimic the appearance and voice of real individuals. This technology has become increasingly accessible and user-friendly, posing significant challenges for detecting and combating deepfake content.

## Potential for Misinformation and Deception

Deepfakes have the potential to be used for malicious purposes, including spreading misinformation, manipulating public opinion, and deceiving individuals. By creating fabricated videos or audio recordings of public figures, politicians, or celebrities, malicious actors can disseminate false or defamatory content to deceive or manipulate audiences. Deepfakes may incite social unrest, undermine trust in institutions, or sow discord within communities.

## Impact on Trust and Authenticity

The proliferation of deepfake technology has eroded trust in the authenticity of audio and video content, making it increasingly challenging for individuals to discern between genuine and manipulated media. As deepfakes become more sophisticated and widespread, the credibility of visual and auditory evidence may be questioned, undermining the integrity of journalism, legal proceedings, and public discourse. This erosion of trust poses significant risks to societal cohesion and democratic norms.

## Challenges for Media Literacy and Verification

Detecting deepfake content presents significant challenges for media literacy and verification efforts. Unlike traditional forms of manipulation, such as photo editing or audio manipulation, deepfakes are often indistinguishable from genuine media to the untrained eye or ear. As a result, individuals may be more susceptible to believing and sharing false information, perpetuating misinformation and disinformation online.

## Ethical and Legal Implications

The proliferation of deepfake technology raises complex ethical and legal questions regarding privacy, consent, and digital media manipulation. The unauthorized use of someone's likeness or voice to create deep fake content may infringe upon their rights and cause harm to their reputation or personal security. Additionally, the malicious dissemination of deepfake content may violate laws against defamation, fraud, or deceptive practices, necessitating legal frameworks to address these emerging threats.

In conclusion, deepfakes and manipulated media pose significant challenges to audio and video content's authenticity, integrity, and trustworthiness in the digital age. Addressing these challenges requires a multifaceted approach that involves technological innovation, media literacy education, regulatory measures, and ethical standards to safeguard against the malicious manipulation of digital media and uphold the integrity of information in society.

# Echo Chambers And Polarization

Echo chambers and polarization represent significant challenges in the contemporary media landscape, fueled partly by Fake News's proliferation and online communication dynamics. Here's an elaboration on these concepts and their implications

## Echo Chambers

An echo chamber is a situation in which individuals are exposed only to information, opinions, or viewpoints that align with their preexisting beliefs or ideologies. In social media and online communities, algorithms and user behavior often create echo chambers by prioritizing content similar to users' previous engagement. As a result, individuals may be insulated from diverse perspectives, alternative viewpoints, or dissenting opinions, reinforcing their existing beliefs and biases.

## Polarization

Social polarization refers to the widening ideological divisions and political polarization within society, where individuals and groups become increasingly divided along partisan lines or ideological fault lines. Echo chambers can exacerbate polarization by fostering an environment in which individuals are exposed only to information that reinforces their beliefs, attitudes, or preferences. This reinforcement can lead to the amplification of ideological differences, the demonization of opposing viewpoints, and a breakdown in civil discourse and mutual understanding.

## Impact on Public Discourse

The prevalence of echo chambers and polarization has significant implications for public discourse, democratic deliberation, and the functioning of civil society. In echo chambers, individuals may be less inclined to critically evaluate information or engage with alternative perspectives, narrowing intellectual curiosity and lacking exposure to diverse viewpoints. This narrowing of discourse can inhibit constructive dialogue, compromise, and consensus-building on critical societal issues, hindering progress and exacerbating social divisions.

## Challenges for Democracy

Echo chambers and polarization challenge democratic governance by undermining the foundations of informed citizenship, civic engagement, and democratic deliberation. In polarized environments, individuals may be more susceptible to manipulation, misinformation, or propaganda reinforcing their beliefs or prejudices. This susceptibility can be exploited by political actors, special interest groups, or malicious actors seeking to influence public opinion, shape electoral outcomes, or undermine democratic institutions.

## Promoting Media Literacy and Critical Thinking

Addressing echo chambers and polarization requires efforts to promote media literacy, critical thinking, and digital citizenship skills among the public. Societies can mitigate the harmful effects of echo chambers and polarization by equipping individuals with the tools to critically evaluate information, discern credible sources from misinformation, and engage in civil discourse with those with different viewpoints. Also, fostering a culture of openness, empathy, and intellectual humility can encourage individuals to seek diverse perspectives, challenge their assumptions, and engage in constructive dialogue across ideological divides.

In conclusion, echo chambers and polarization represent significant challenges for contemporary society, undermining the quality of public discourse, democratic governance, and social cohesion. By promoting media literacy, fostering diverse viewpoints, and cultivating a culture of civil discourse and mutual respect, societies can mitigate the harmful effects of echo chambers and polarization, fostering a more inclusive, informed, and democratic public sphere.

# Global Disinformation Campaigns

Global disinformation campaigns threaten democratic institutions, geopolitical stability, and public trust in information sources. Here's an elaboration on the nature and implications of such campaigns

## Coordinated Efforts

Global disinformation campaigns involve coordinated efforts by state actors, non-state actors, or other entities to spread false or misleading information on a massive scale. These campaigns often leverage a combination of traditional propaganda tactics and modern digital tools and platforms to reach target audiences and amplify their messaging. They may involve the creation of Fake News websites, social media accounts, or online communities dedicated to spreading misinformation and influencing public opinion.

## Undermining Democratic Institutions

The primary objective of global disinformation campaigns is often to undermine democratic institutions, sow division, and weaken the social fabric of target countries. By spreading false narratives, amplifying existing grievances, and exploiting societal fault lines, foreign actors seek to erode public trust in democratic processes, institutions, and leaders. This can lead to heightened political polarization, social unrest, and a loss of confidence in the integrity of electoral systems and democratic governance.

## Geopolitical Objectives

Global disinformation campaigns are often driven by geopolitical considerations, with foreign actors seeking to advance their strategic interests and undermine rivals on the world stage. These campaigns may target countries perceived as geopolitical adversaries or competitors, seeking to exploit internal divisions and weaken their influence on the global stage. By sowing chaos, confusion, and distrust, foreign actors can disrupt democratic processes, destabilize governments, and create opportunities to advance their agendas.

## Implications for National Security

The proliferation of global disinformation campaigns poses significant national security and defense challenges. False or misleading information can manipulate public opinion, incite social unrest, or undermine confidence in government institutions and leaders. In a hybrid and information warfare era, disinformation campaigns can weaken adversaries, undermine alliances, and achieve strategic objectives without resorting to traditional military force.

## Addressing the Threat

Addressing the threat of global disinformation requires a coordinated and multi-dimensional response involving governments, tech companies, civil society organizations, and the media. This may include efforts to enhance cybersecurity, strengthen resilience against information warfare, promote media literacy and critical thinking skills, and improve transparency and accountability in the online information ecosystem. International cooperation and information sharing are also essential for effectively identifying and countering foreign disinformation operations.

In conclusion, global disinformation campaigns significantly challenge democratic governance, national security, and global stability. By understanding the nature and implications of these campaigns and implementing robust measures to counter them, societies can better defend against the spread of false information and safeguard the integrity of democratic institutions and processes.

# Critical Thinking And Media Literacy

Critical thinking and media literacy are indispensable tools in the modern era, where the proliferation of Fake News and misinformation poses significant challenges to informed decision-making and democratic discourse. Here's an elaboration on the importance and implications of promoting critical thinking and media literacy

## Empowering Individuals

Critical thinking and media literacy empower individuals to navigate the vast and often complex information landscape with discernment and skepticism. By developing the ability to evaluate sources, analyze arguments, and question assumptions, individuals can make informed judgments about the credibility and reliability of information encountered online, in the media, and everyday life.

## Combatting misinformation

Media literacy education is crucial in combating misinformation and disinformation by equipping individuals with the skills and knowledge to identify and critically evaluate false or misleading information. By teaching individuals how to recognize standard propaganda techniques, logical fallacies, and manipulation tactics, media literacy education enables them to distinguish between credible and unreliable information sources.

## Promoting Civic Engagement

Critical thinking and media literacy are essential for promoting civic engagement and participation in a democratic society. Informed citizens who critically evaluate information are better equipped to engage in meaningful dialogue, participate in public discourse, and hold elected officials and institutions accountable. Media literacy education fosters active citizenship by encouraging individuals to question authority, seek diverse perspectives, and make evidence-based decisions.

## Fostering Resilience to Manipulation

By developing critical thinking skills and media literacy competencies, individuals become more resilient to manipulation and propaganda. They are less susceptible to being swayed by false narratives, conspiracy theories, and sensationalized content to exploit cognitive biases and emotional triggers. Media literacy education empowers individuals to resist manipulation and make rational, evidence-based judgments about the information they encounter.

## Building a Culture of Skepticism

Critical thinking and media literacy education contribute to developing a culture of skepticism and inquiry, where individuals are encouraged to question assumptions, challenge authority, and seek out reliable information in a society where misinformation is pervasive, fostering a healthy skepticism towards information sources and claims is essential for maintaining intellectual integrity and intellectual autonomy.

## Promoting Lifelong Learning

Media literacy education is not just about acquiring skills; it's about cultivating a mindset of curiosity, inquiry, and lifelong learning. By instilling a habit of critical inquiry and intellectual curiosity, media literacy education prepares individuals to adapt to the ever-changing information landscape and engage critically with new technologies, platforms, and media formats.

In conclusion, promoting critical thinking and media literacy is essential for empowering individuals to navigate the complexities of the information age, combat misinformation, and participate meaningfully in a democratic society. By investing in media literacy education and fostering a culture of skepticism and inquiry, societies can equip citizens with the tools to discern truth from falsehood and make informed decisions in an increasingly interconnected and information-rich world.

# Collaborative Efforts

Addressing the multifaceted challenges of Fake News requires collaborative efforts involving governments, technology companies, civil society organizations, and the media. Multi-stakeholder approaches that leverage expertise from diverse sectors can enhance information integrity, promote digital literacy, and strengthen democratic resilience against the spread of Fake News and disinformation.

Collaborative efforts are paramount in tackling the complex and evolving threat of Fake News. Here's an elaboration on the importance and benefits of collaborative approaches

## Pooling Resources and Expertise

Governments, technology companies, civil society organizations, and the media bring unique perspectives, resources, and expertise. Collaborative efforts enable these stakeholders to pool their resources, share insights, and leverage their respective strengths to develop comprehensive strategies for combating Fake News. By drawing on diverse perspectives and skill sets, collaborative initiatives can generate innovative solutions that address the root causes of misinformation and disinformation.

## Coordinated Action

Fake News is a global phenomenon that transcends national borders and jurisdictions. Collaborative efforts facilitate coordinated action at the international, national, and local levels to address the spread of Fake News effectively. By sharing information, coordinating responses, and aligning policies and regulations, stakeholders can create a united front against Fake News and disinformation campaigns that seek to undermine democratic institutions and values.

## Promoting Digital Literacy

Digital literacy is essential for equipping individuals with the skills and knowledge to navigate the digital landscape safely and responsibly. Collaborative efforts can enhance digital literacy initiatives by bringing educators, policymakers, tech companies, and community organizations together to develop and implement educational programs, resources, and campaigns that promote critical thinking, media literacy, and digital citizenship skills. By working together, stakeholders can reach broader audiences and create more impactful educational interventions.

## Building Trust and Transparency

Collaboration fosters trust and transparency among stakeholders, which is critical for effective communication, information-sharing, and coordination. By engaging in open dialogue, building relationships, and establishing mechanisms for collaboration and accountability, stakeholders can build trust with each other and the public. Transparency about goals, processes, and outcomes helps foster credibility and legitimacy, ensuring that collaborative efforts are perceived as credible and effective by stakeholders and the broader community.

## Adapting to Emerging Threats

Fake News is a constantly evolving threat that requires agile and adaptive responses. Collaborative efforts enable stakeholders to monitor emerging trends, share intelligence, and respond rapidly to new threats and challenges. By staying vigilant and proactive, stakeholders can identify emerging disinformation tactics, develop countermeasures, and adapt strategies to mitigate the impact of Fake News on society.

In conclusion, collaborative efforts are essential for addressing the multifaceted challenges of Fake News and disinformation. By pooling resources, coordinating action, promoting digital literacy, building trust, and adapting to emerging threats, stakeholders can enhance information integrity, strengthen democratic resilience, and safeguard the public against the harmful effects of Fake News and disinformation.

## In Summary

By considering these additional aspects of the Fake News phenomenon, we can develop more nuanced and comprehensive strategies for addressing the challenges of misinformation and safeguarding the integrity of public discourse and democratic processes.

Addressing the challenges of misinformation requires a multifaceted approach that considers various aspects of the Fake News phenomenon. By examining these additional dimensions, we can develop more nuanced and comprehensive strategies to combat misinformation and safeguard the integrity of public discourse and democratic processes.

# Spot the Fake News

Distinguishing Fake News from real news is very important today. Here are some tips to help you spot Fake News

## Check the Source

"Check the Source" means you should always look at where the news is coming from. Trusted news sources, like well-known newspapers and TV channels, usually have a good reputation for telling the truth. They have a history of reliable reporting, meaning they have consistently provided accurate information over time.

How to Check the Source

### Recognize Trusted Names

If the news is from well-known sources like The New York Times, BBC, or CNN, it's more likely to be reliable. These organizations have teams of journalists who check their facts.

### Research Unknow Sources

If you find a news article from a website you haven't heard of, take a few minutes to research it. Look up the website and see what others say about it. You can search for reviews or check sites like Media Bias/Fact Check to see if it's considered trustworthy.

### Look at the Website's About Page

Reliable news websites usually have an "About" page that tells you who runs the site, what their mission is, and who their reporters are. It could be a red flag if this information is missing or vague.

## Check for Contact Information

Legitimate news sites usually have contact information available. This includes addresses, phone numbers, and email addresses. Fake news sites might not provide this information.

## Review the Writing Style

Professional news sources follow journalistic standards, including proper grammar, straightforward language, and a neutral tone. If the writing seems unprofessional, it might not be a reliable source.

## Check for Ads and Pop-Ups

Reliable news sites usually have a clean, professional look. Suppose a website is cluttered with ads and pop-ups. In that case, it might be more interested in making money than providing accurate news.

## Verify with Other Sources

See if other reputable news organizations are reporting the same story. It might not be accurate if only one website has the news and others don't.

By checking your news source, you can ensure that the information you're getting is accurate and trustworthy. This helps you avoid being misled by Fake News.

# Look at the Author

"Look at the Author" means you should find out who wrote the article to help decide if the news is real. Here's how you can do that

How to Check the Author

## Find the Author's Name

Look for the author's name, usually listed at the beginning or end of the article. Real news stories usually include the author's name.

## Research the Author

Once you have the author's name, search for them online. See if they have written other articles and what topics they cover. Good authors usually have a history of writing for respected news outlets.

## Check for a Journalist Profile

Many journalists have profiles on the news website where they work. These profiles often include their experience, past work, and areas of expertise. If the author has a profile, it shows they are a real journalist.

## Look at Their Social Media

Many journalists are active on social media platforms like Twitter or LinkedIn. Check if they have professional accounts where they share news updates and engage with other journalists. This can give you an idea of their credibility.

## Assess Their Credentials

See if the author has a background in journalism or a related field. Reliable journalists usually have degrees in journalism, communications, or similar areas. They might also have won awards or received recognition for their work.

## Check for Anonymous Authors

Be careful if an article doesn't list an author. While there can be valid reasons for anonymity, Fake News often doesn't list an author. No author makes it harder to check the article's credibility.

## Review Past Work

Look at other articles the author has written. See if they follow journalistic standards like citing sources, providing evidence, and keeping a neutral tone. Consistently good work is a sign of a reliable author.

## Be Wary of Unknown Authors

If the author has no background in journalism or only appears on sketchy websites, be cautious. An unknown or unverified author might not provide trustworthy information.

By looking at the author, you can better judge if the article is reliable. Authors with solid journalism backgrounds are more likely to write accurate and trustworthy news.

# Examine the Date

"Examine the Date" means you should always check when the news article was published. This helps you make sure the information is current and relevant. Here's how you can do that

How to Examine the Date

## Find the Publication Date

Look for the date when the article was published. This is usually found near the author's name at the beginning or end of the article.

## Check for Updates

Some articles are updated after they are first published. Look for a note that says when the article was last updated. This is important because the information might have changed since it was first written.

## Compare with Current Events

Make sure the news matches with what is currently happening. Old news can sometimes be shared as if it's new, which can confuse people. For example, a report about an election from several years ago might be shared again, making it seem like it's about a current election.

## Look for Context Clues

Sometimes, the article might mention dates within the text. Pay attention to these details to understand when the events took place.

## Be Cautious with Old News

If you find the news old, consider whether it's still relevant. Some information, like scientific discoveries, might still be helpful, even if it's not recent. However, other information, like weather forecasts or breaking news, quickly becomes outdated.

## Avoid Misinformation

Sharing old news as if it's new can spread misinformation. For example, an old health warning might cause unnecessary panic if people think it's a new threat.

## Consider the Time Lag

Sometimes, news can be reported later than when the event happened. Check if there is a delay between the event and the publication date, and consider why that might happen.

Examining the date ensures that the news you're reading is current and relevant, helping you avoid confusion and misinformation.

# Read Beyond the Headline

"Read Beyond the Headline" means you should not rely on the headline to understand the news. Headlines can sometimes be sensational or misleading. Here's how to do this

How to Read Beyond the Headline

## Understand the Headline's Purpose

Headlines are designed to grab your attention quickly. Sometimes, they use solid or emotional language to make you click on the article.

## Read the Full Article

After seeing the headline, take the time to read the entire article. The details and context in the full text will give you a better understanding of the story.

## Look for Key Information

The full article looks for important information like who, what, when, where, why, and how. This helps you get the complete picture of the news story.

## Identify the Main Points

Summarize the main points of the article. This helps ensure you understand the key details and are not just influenced by the headline.

## Check for Quotes and Sources

Reliable articles often include quotes from experts or witnesses and cite their sources. This adds credibility to the information and provides evidence for the claims made.

## Be Aware of Sensationalism

Some headlines are designed to provoke strong emotions like fear or anger. The actual article might be less dramatic and more balanced. You can see if the headline was exaggerated by reading the full article.

## Understand the Context

Headlines can sometimes take information out of context. The full article usually explains the background and context of the story, helping you understand why something happened and what it means.

## Recognize Clickbait

Clickbait headlines are specifically designed to get clicks, often at the expense of accuracy. These headlines can be misleading or only tell part of the story. Reading the whole article helps you avoid falling for clickbait.

## Analyze the Author's Intention

Sometimes, headlines are written to push a specific viewpoint or bias. By reading the full article, you can better assess the author's intentions and whether the information is presented fairly.

## Discuss and Share Thoughtfully

Before sharing news with others, ensure you've read and understood the full article. This helps prevent the spread of misinformation and ensures you share accurate information.

By reading beyond the headline, you can better understand the news and avoid being misled by sensational or incomplete information.

# Check the Facts

"Check the Facts" means verifying the information in a news article to ensure it is accurate and reliable. Real news stories are based on facts and evidence, while Fake News often lacks this. Here's how to do it

How to Check the Facts

## Look for Data and Statistics

Reliable news articles often include data and statistics to support their claims. Check if these numbers are sourced from credible organizations or studies.

## Identify Quotes and Sources

Check if the article includes quotes from experts, witnesses, or officials. Reliable news stories cite their sources, providing names and sometimes titles or organizations.

## Verify Sources

If the article cites sources, see if you can verify them independently. Look up the experts or organizations mentioned to see if they are reputable.

## Cross-Check Information

Compare the information in the article with other reputable news sources. If multiple reliable sources report the same facts, the information is more likely to be accurate.

## Check for References

Some articles link to sources, such as studies, reports, or official statements. Follow these links to see if the information matches what the article says.

## Use Fact-Checking Websites

Websites like Snopes, FactCheck.org, and PolitiFact specialize in verifying news stories and claims. Check these sites to see if they have evaluated the article or similar claims.

## Look for Detailed Evidence

Reliable news stories provide detailed evidence and explanations. Be cautious if the article makes big claims but offers little evidence or vague details.

## Beware of Misleading Information

Sometimes, articles can use accurate data but present it misleadingly. Look for context and see if the article explains the data thoroughly and accurately.

## Understand the Methodology

If the article includes a study or poll, check if it explains the methodology. Reliable studies usually provide details on how the data was collected and analyzed.

## Check Author Credibility

Sometimes, the credibility of the author can also be a clue. Suppose the author has a history of reliable reporting and fact-based journalism. In that case, their articles are more likely to be accurate.

## Look for Peer Reviews

For scientific and academic articles, check if the information has been peer-reviewed. This means other experts have evaluated and approved the research.

By checking the facts, you can ensure that the news you read is based on solid evidence, not just rumors or opinions. This helps you stay well-informed and avoid spreading false information.

# Look for Multiple Sources

"Look for Multiple Sources" means checking if various reliable news outlets report a news story. This can help you determine if the information is accurate and trustworthy. Here's how you can do that
    How to Look for Multiple Sources

## Search for the Story

Use a search engine to look up the news story. See if multiple reputable news websites are reporting the same information.

## Compare Different Outlets

Check various news sources, such as well-known newspapers, TV, and online news sites. Reliable news is usually covered by several of these outlets.

## Check International Sources

Sometimes, looking at international news sources can provide additional verification. Major news organizations around the world often report on significant events.

## Look for Consistency

See if the main facts of the story are consistent across different sources. If the key details match, the story will likely be accurate.

## Beware of Unique Stories

Be cautious if only one news outlet reports the story and no one else has picked it up. It might be an exclusive scoop, but it could also be fake or exaggerated.

## Verify with Official Sources

Check if official sources like government agencies, companies, or organizations confirm the story. Official statements can add credibility to the news.

## Use News Aggregators

Websites and apps aggregating news from various sources can help you quickly see which stories are widely reported. Examples include Google News and Apple News.

## Check for Press Releases

Sometimes, news stories are based on press releases from companies or organizations. Look for these press releases to see if the news is directly sourced from an official announcement.

## Follow Up

Reliable news outlets often provide updates as new information becomes available. Follow the story over time to see if it continues to be reported and verified by multiple sources.

## Consider the Source's Reputation

Established news organizations with a history of reliable reporting are more trustworthy. If several reputable sources report the same story, it adds credibility.

## Check for Expert Opinions

Sometimes, experts in the field will comment on or verify the news. Look for these expert opinions to confirm the story further.

By looking for multiple sources, you can better assess the reliability of a news story. When various reputable outlets report the same information, it's more likely to be true. This helps you avoid being misled by fake or exaggerated news.

# Analyze the Tone

"Analyze the Tone" means examining how an article is written to help determine its reliability. Authentic news articles typically have a neutral and factual tone. In contrast, Fake News often uses emotional or strong language to provoke reactions. Here's how to analyze the tone of a news article

How to Analyze the Tone

## Look for Emotional Language

Check if the article uses words that evoke strong emotions like fear, anger, or joy. Phrases like "shocking truth," "amazing discovery," or "outrageous behavior" are often used to grab attention and may indicate a lack of objectivity.

## Assess the Neutrality

Real news aims to present facts without taking sides. If the article seems biased or one-sided, presenting only one perspective, it may not be a reliable source.

## Check for Adjectives and Adverbs

Articles with lots of descriptive words might influence your opinion rather than inform you. Words like "disgraceful," "horrific," or "brilliant" can indicate bias.

## Identify Persuasive Techniques

Look for techniques like hyperbole (exaggeration), sensationalism, or scare tactics. These are often used in Fake News to manipulate readers' emotions and reactions.

## Evaluate the Objectivity

Authentic news articles provide evidence and multiple viewpoints. Be cautious if the article seems more like an opinion piece without clear evidence.

## Consider the Structure

Reliable news articles usually follow a structured format, initially providing the most crucial information and supporting details later. Articles with many personal opinions or anecdotal evidence may be less trustworthy.

## Look for Loaded Questions

Be wary of questions that assume something controversial or present information in a biased way, like "Why is the government hiding the truth?" These questions can be misleading and suggest a lack of objectivity.

## Check the Sources' Tone

Evaluate the tone of quotes and sources used in the article. Reliable sources use factual language, while questionable sources might use more emotional or sensational language.

## Analyze Headlines and Subheadings

Headlines and subheadings should accurately reflect the content of the article. Sensational or misleading headlines are a red flag.

## Be Wary of Absolutes

Phrases like "always," "never," "everyone," or "no one" can be signs of exaggeration. Real news is usually more nuanced and avoids making sweeping generalizations.

## Consider the Purpose

Think about why the article was written. Is it to inform, persuade, entertain, or provoke? News articles should aim to inform with clear, evidence-based reporting.

By analyzing the tone of a news article, you can better assess its credibility. Real news maintains a neutral and factual tone, avoiding emotional language and bias. This helps you make more informed decisions and avoid being misled by Fake News.

# Verify Images and Videos

"Verify Images and Videos" means checking the authenticity of visual media in news stories to ensure they have not been altered or taken out of context. Here's how you can do that

How to Verify Images and Videos

## Use Reverse Image Search Tools

Google Reverse Image Search

Upload the image or paste its URL into the Google Images search bar. This tool will show you where else the image appears online.

TinEye

Like Google, TinEye lets you search for images to see where and how they've been used on the internet.

## Check for Manipulations

Look closely at the image for signs of editing. This can include unusual shadows, inconsistent lighting, or pixelation around objects or people. Tools like Photoshop can help identify these manipulations, but even a careful visual inspection can reveal apparent edits.

## Analyze the Context

Images and videos can be taken out of context to mislead. Try to find the original source of the media and see the context in which it was initially used. This helps ensure the media is being presented accurately in the current story.

## Look for Metadata

Metadata is information embedded in media files that can provide details about when and where an image or video was taken. Tools like ExifTool can help you extract and analyze this metadata, though be aware that metadata can also be manipulated.

## Use Video Verification Tools

Tools like InVID or Amnesty International's YouTube DataViewer can help verify video authenticity. These tools break down videos into keyframes and help you search for these frames online to check for previous uses.

## Check for Logos and Watermarks

Some images and videos have logos or watermarks indicating their source. Verify that these match the claimed source of the media. If a watermark has been tampered with or removed, it could be a sign of manipulation.

## Compare with Trusted Sources

Check if reputable news outlets use the image or video. Trusted sources often have teams that verify media before publication. If they are using the same media, it's more likely to be authentic.

## Look for Related Media

Sometimes, multiple photos or videos are taken at the same event. Look for other media from the same time and place to confirm the authenticity and context of the image or video.

## Use Fact-Checking Websites

Websites like Snopes, FactCheck.org, and others often investigate viral images and videos. They provide detailed analyses and conclusions about the authenticity of the media.

## Be Skeptical of Viral Media

Media that goes viral quickly can often be misleading or altered to provoke strong reactions. Approach viral images and videos carefully and verify them thoroughly before believing or sharing.

By verifying images and videos, you can avoid being misled by altered or out-of-context media. This helps ensure you get the true story and not a distorted version designed to deceive.

# Consider Bias

"Consider Bias" means being aware that all news sources have some degree of bias, and recognizing extreme bias can help you avoid Fake News. Here's how to consider bias effectively

How to Consider Bias

# Understand Different Types of Bias

Political Bias

This occurs when news sources favor a particular political party or viewpoint.

Cultural Bias

Some news outlets may lean toward specific cultural perspectives or values.

Commercial Bias

News organizations may favor stories that attract more viewers or advertisers.

# Identify the Source's Bias

Research the Outlet

Look up the history and ownership of the news outlet. Knowing who owns the outlet and their affiliations can provide insight into potential biases.

Check Bias Ratings

Websites like Media Bias/Fact Check, AllSides, and Ad Fontes Media rate the bias of various news outlets, helping you identify where a source might lean.

## Analyze Language and Tone

Loaded Language

Words that carry solid emotional implications can indicate bias. For example, "heroic" or "tyrannical" suggests a strong bias toward or against the subject.

Framing

Notice how the story is framed. Is it presenting one side as clearly right or wrong? Balanced stories typically present multiple viewpoints.

## Examine Source Selection

Diverse Sources

A balanced article will cite multiple sources from different perspectives. It may not be very objective if an article only quotes people from one side.

Omission

Be aware of what's left out. Sometimes, bias is evident in what is not reported as much as in what is.

# Look for Opinion vs. Fact

## Clear Distinction

Reputable news sources clearly distinguish between news reports and opinion pieces. It might be biased if an article mixes opinion with fact without clear separation.

## Editorials and Columns

Understand that editorials and opinion columns are meant to express viewpoints and are inherently biased.

# Read from Multiple Sources

## Diverse Perspectives

Read news from outlets with different biases to get a well-rounded view. For instance, if you read something from a conservative outlet, also check a liberal one to see how they report the same story.

## Compare Coverage

See how different outlets cover the same story. Differences in reporting can highlight biases and help you find the most accurate information.

# Be Aware of Confirmation Bias

## Challenge Your Views

Seek out news that challenges your own beliefs. This helps you understand different perspectives and avoid only consuming news that confirms your preexisting views.

## Critical Thinking

Question all news, even from sources you trust. Critical thinking helps you identify bias and understand the full context.

# Recognize Extreme Bias

## Hyperbolic Language

Extreme bias often involves exaggerated or hyperbolic language. Be wary of articles that use dramatic language without evidence.

## One-Sided Reporting

If a source consistently presents one side of every story and dismisses the other, it might be highly biased.

# Consider the Purpose

## Inform or Persuade?

Determine if the article aims to inform or persuade. News should primarily aim to inform, while biased articles often try to persuade the reader to adopt a specific viewpoint.

Reflect on Your Own Bias

Self-Awareness

Be aware of your biases and how they might influence how you perceive news. Strive for an objective approach when evaluating different sources.

By considering bias, you can critically assess the information you consume, ensuring you get a more balanced and accurate view of the news. This helps you avoid being influenced by Fake News and extreme biases.

# Check for Satire

"Check for Satire" means verifying whether a news story is intended to be humorous or a parody rather than actual news. Satirical websites publish content meant to entertain or critique through humor, and it's essential to recognize these to avoid mistaking them for real news. Here's how to check for satire

How to Check for Satire

## Know Common Satirical Sites

Famous Satire Websites

Be familiar with well-known satire websites like The Onion, The Babylon Bee, and ClickHole. These sites create humorous, exaggerated stories that are not meant to be taken seriously.

Look for Site Labels

Some satire sites clearly label themselves as satire or parody. Check the website's "About" page or disclaimers for this information.

## Examine the Content

### Exaggerated Claims

Satirical articles often make exaggerated or absurd claims that seem too outlandish to be true. If the story sounds ridiculous, it might be satire.

### Humorous Tone

Satirical stories are usually written in a humorous, sarcastic, or ironic tone. If the article is trying to make you laugh or is obviously mocking someone or something, it's likely satire.

## Check the Author and Site Information

### Author Bios

Look at the author's bio. On satirical sites, authors often have humorous or fictitious biographies that hint at the nature of their work.

### Website Reputation

Research the website's reputation. A quick online search can reveal whether the site is known for publishing satire.

## Look for Context Clues

### Website Sections

Satirical sites often have sections dedicated to different types of humor or parody. Check if the article is listed under a humor or satire section.

Visual Cues

Satirical articles may include humorous images, cartoons, or memes that add to the comedic tone.

## Cross-check with Other Sources

Verify with Reliable News

See if reputable news sources report the story. Multiple credible outlets usually cover real news stories, while satire is not.

Fact-Checking Websites

Websites like Snopes and FactCheck.org often identify and explain satirical stories that have been mistaken for real news.

## Read the Fine Print

Disclaimers

Some satire sites include disclaimers at the bottom of the page or within the article stating that the content is fictional and meant for entertainment.

## Understand the Purpose of Satire

Critique and Humor

Satire aims to critique society, politics, and culture through humor. Recognize that these articles aim not to inform but to entertain or provoke thought.

## Be Skeptical of Viral Stories

Viral Satire

Sometimes, satirical stories go viral and are shared out of context. Approach sensational or highly shared stories with caution and verify their authenticity.

You can distinguish between humorous, fictional content and real news by checking for satire. This helps you avoid being misled and ensures you are informed by accurate, reliable information.

By following these steps, you can better distinguish between Fake News and accurate news and stay well-informed.

# Don't miss out!

Visit the website below and you can sign up to receive emails whenever Adrian Rocquecliffe publishes a new book. There's no charge and no obligation.

https://books2read.com/r/B-A-LUNRB-FVCQD

BOOKS 2 READ

Connecting independent readers to independent writers.

Did you love *Extra! Extra! Read All About It*? Then you should read *Making America Great Altogether - Call to Action*[1] by Adrian Rocquecliffe!

[2]

In our rallying cry, 'Making America Great Altogether – Call to Action,' unity takes center stage but with a twist. Instead of pushing for uniformity, we celebrate the vibrant patchwork of perspectives that make up our nation. It's about inclusivity, where every voice, no matter how different, is not just heard but cherished. This is not just a call. It's an invitation to be part of something bigger.

This call for unity recognizes that diversity isn't just a buzzword—it's the lifeblood of progress. By weaving together the varied threads of American society, we create a tapestry of resilience and innovation. Whether you're from a bustling city or a quiet country town, whether

---

1. https://books2read.com/u/mK25PP

2. https://books2read.com/u/mK25PP

your roots trace back generations or you're a newcomer, your voice matters. You are an integral part of this collective progress.

But it's not just about warm fuzzies; it's practical, too. In a world where challenges come fast and furious, we need all hands on deck. By embracing our differences and fostering a culture of openness, we tap into a wellspring of creativity and insight that can steer us through even the toughest of times.

Let's ditch the divisiveness and roll out the welcome mat for all. In "Making America Great Altogether," we're not just talking the talk; we're walking the walk toward a future where everyone has a seat at the table.

Read more at https://www.makingamericagreataltogether.us/adrian_rocquecliffe.

# Also by Adrian Rocquecliffe

Making America Great Altogether - Call to Action
Trump's Vision of MAGA- The Fallacy
Extra! Extra! Read All About It

Watch for more at https://www.makingamericagreataltogether.us/adrian_rocquecliffe.

# About the Author

Adrian Rocquecliffe's journey from a young boy navigating cultural divides to a successful entrepreneur and visionary leader exemplifies the American dream. His dedication to improving the country for future generations is a testament to his belief in the power of unity and collaboration. As he continues his work with "Making America Great Altogether," Adrian remains hopeful that his efforts will contribute to a better, more inclusive America when he retires.

Read more at https://www.makingamericagreataltogether.us/adrian_rocquecliffe.